Helen Mortimer & Cristina Trapa...

Doing Your Best

OXFORD
UNIVERSITY PRESS

Be yourself

Everybody is different and to do your best, first you have to be yourself.

Aim high

Set yourself a goal—and enjoy the feeling when you reach it!

Challenge

If we never challenge ourselves,
we will never really know
what we are able
to do.

Learn

Never be afraid of making mistakes.

When something goes wrong, it helps us
to learn how to do it better next time.

Build

It's worth spending time
to build your plans,
hopes and dreams.

PLAN

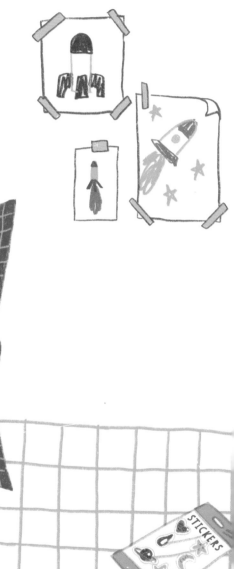

Practise

Don't give up, keep trying, practise every day—it's all part of your journey.

Teamwork

Sometimes you need others to help
help you to improve and succeed.

When you work as a team, you can achieve things together.

Positive

When we feel positive and
powerful . . . we shine!

Confidence

If you believe in yourself and remember all the energy and focus you have put into something, it will show.

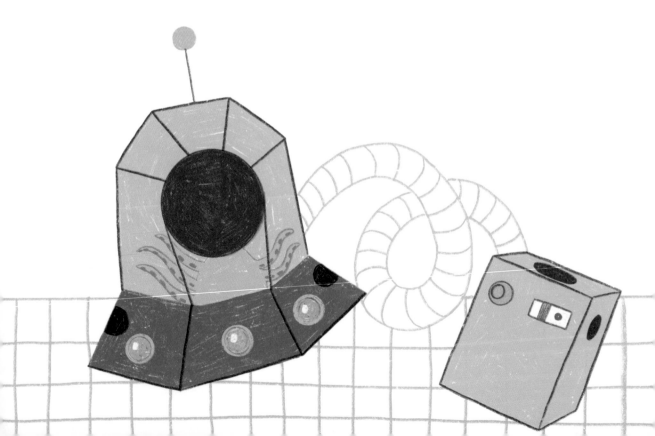

Praise

It feels good when someone gives us praise.

So remember to
encourage your friends!

Proud

You should feel proud of yourself,
because you are amazing!

Doing your best

If you follow your dreams and go for it, you will be doing your best!

Ten ideas for getting the most from this book

1 Take your time. Sharing a book gives you a precious chance to experience something together and provides so many things to talk about.

2 This book is all about doing your best. You can do your best even with the simplest things, like brushing your teeth. Can you think of something you did today where you tried your hardest?

3 It's also a book about language. Ask each other what words you would use to describe doing your best.

4 The illustrations in this book capture various moments as five children get ready for a show. Why not suggest what might have happened just before each moment and what might happen next?

5 Would you like to be in the show, too? What would you like to do the most—sing, play an instrument, juggle, dance, or make the costumes?

6 Try to get inside the heads and hearts of each child. How do they make sure that they do their best?

7 This book also recognizes that sometimes things go wrong . . . and that making mistakes is all part of doing your best.

8 By exploring the ways we can describe and express doing our best, we hope this book will give children and the adults in their lives the tools they need to make sense of themselves and the world around them.

9 The show has an outer space theme. Astronauts have to do their best to train for going into space. What would you like to do when you grow up and how will you try to reach your dream?

10 You could each choose a favourite word about doing your best from the book—it will probably be different each time you share the story!

Glossary

achieve – if you achieve something, you manage to do it

challenge – if we challenge ourselves, we try to do something new and exciting but also difficult

goal – something to aim for

improve – when you improve, you get better at doing something

positive – when we feel positive, we are hopeful about something